zendoodle coloring

Cozy Cats

Other great books in the series

zendoodle coloring

Calming Swirls

Creative Sensations

Enchanting Gardens

Inspiring Zendalas

Into the Forest

zendoodle coloring

Cozy Cats

Fantastic Felines to Color and Display

illustrations by

Nikolett Corley

ST. MARTIN'S GRIFFIN
NEW YORK

ZENDOODLE COLORING: COZY CATS.

Printed in the United States of America. For information, address
St. Martin's Press, 175 Fifth Avenue, New York, N.Y. 10010.

www.stmartins.com

ISBN 978-1-250-10878-4 (trade paperback)

Our books may be purchased in bulk for promotional, educational, or business use.
Please contact your local bookseller or the Macmillan Corporate and Premium
Sales Department at 1-800-221-7945, extension 5442, or by e-mail
at MacmillanSpecialMarkets@macmillan.com.

First Edition: March 2016

10 9 8 7 6 5 4 3 2

PHOTO
1000S

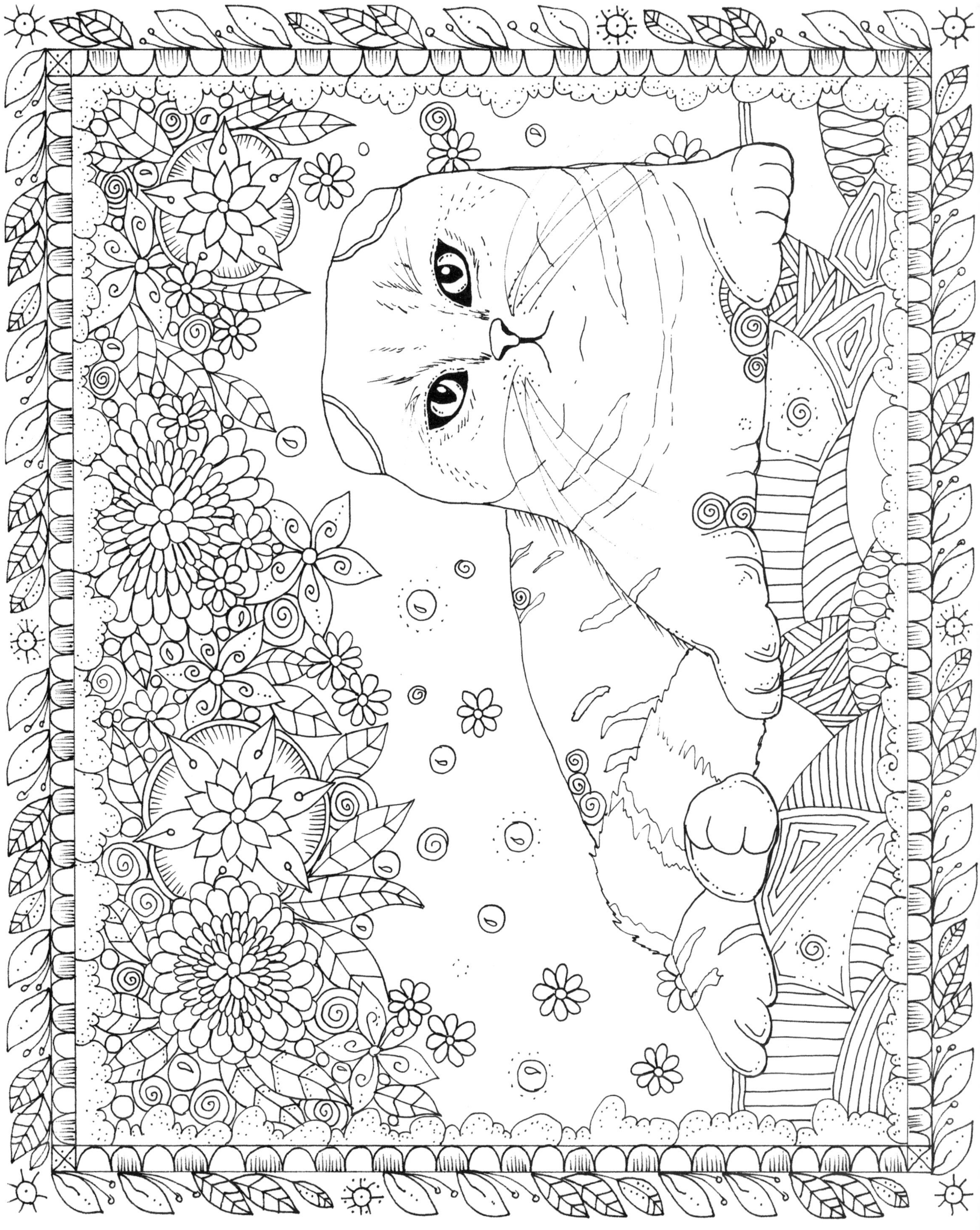

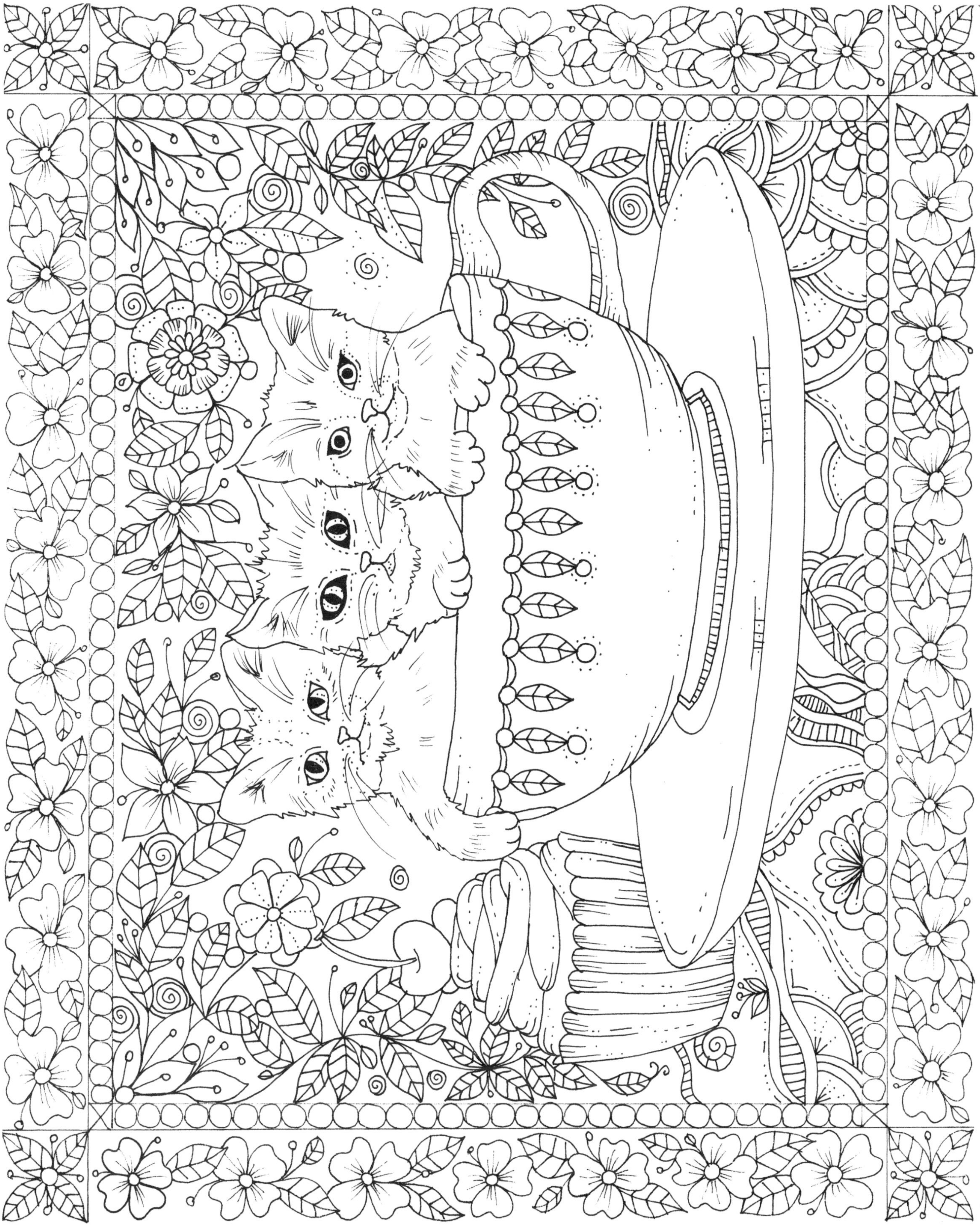

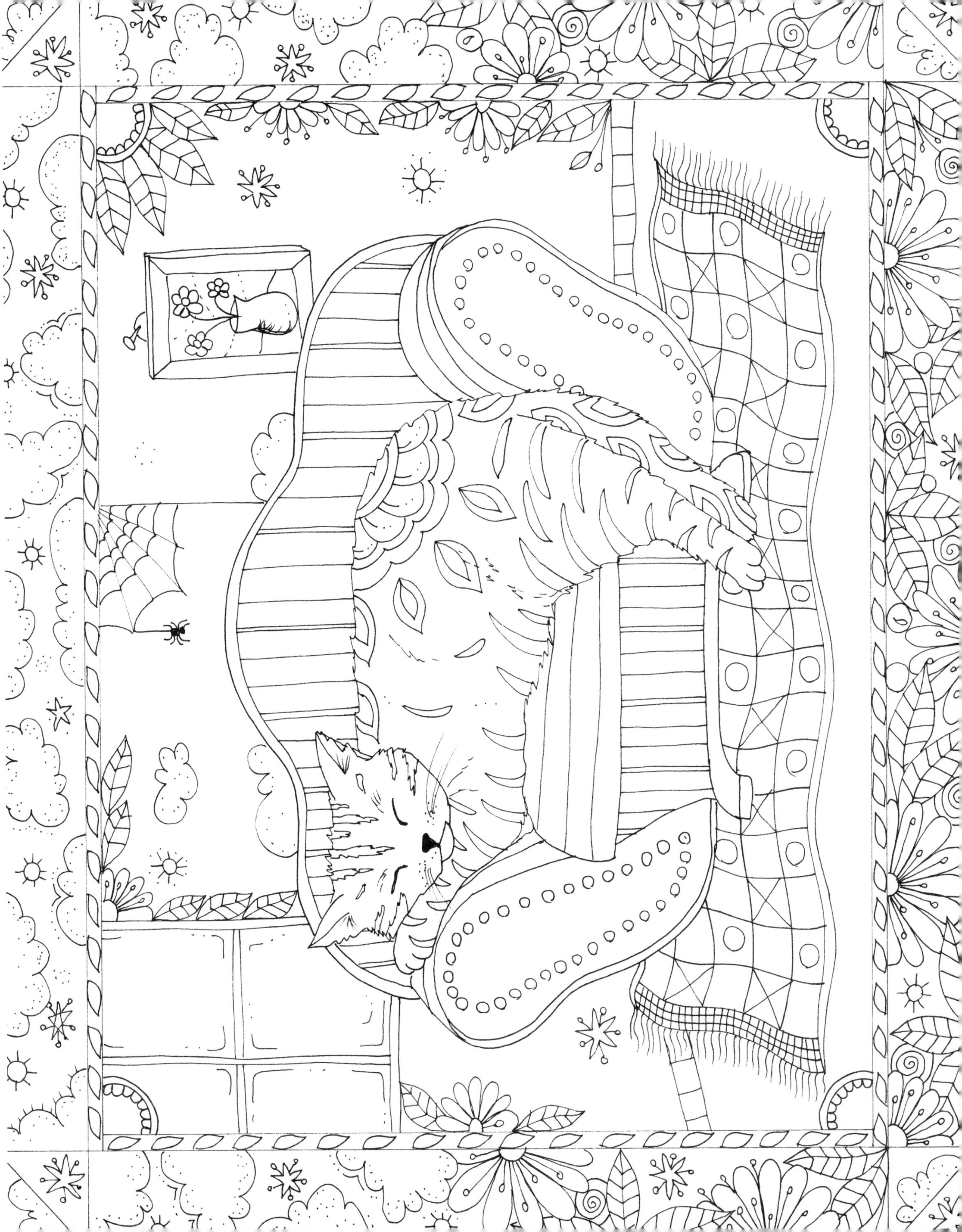